X-treme DISASTERS

THAT CHANGED AMERICA

DUST BOWL!

The 1930s Black Blizzards

by Richard H. Levey

Consultant: Daniel H. Franck, Ph.D.

BEARPORT

PUBLISHING COMPANY, INC.

New York, New York

Credits

Cover, Library of Congress Prints & Photographs Collection, Underwood Archives, Bettman / CORBIS.

Title page, Library of Congress Prints & Photographs Collection; 4-5, Franklin D. Roosevelt Presidential Library and Museum; 6, 7, Courtesy of the National Oceanic and Atmospheric Administration Central Library Photo Collection; 9, Bettmann / CORBIS; 10-11, Monica Ponomarev; 11, United States Department of Agriculture Photo Library; 12-13, CORBIS; 14, CORBIS; 15, Library of Congress Prints & Photographs Collection; 16-17, 18-19, CORBIS; 20, Underwood Archives; 21, Photo courtesy of USDA Natural Resources Conservation Service; 22, Library of Congress Prints & Photographs Collection; 23, CORBIS; 24-25, Underwood Archives; 25, Russell Lee / Getty Images; 26-27, Scott Bauer / Agricultural Research Service / United States Department Agriculture; 26, Bettmann / CORBIS; 29, Franklin D. Roosevelt Presidential Library and Museum.

Design and production by Dawn Beard Creative, Triesta Hall of Blu-Design, and Octavo Design and Production, Inc.

Library of Congress Cataloging-in-Publication Data

Levey, Richard H.
 Dust bowl! : the 1930s black blizzards / by Richard H. Levey ; consultant, Daniel H. Franck.
   p. cm. — (X-treme disasters that changed America)
 Includes bibliographical references and index.
 ISBN 1-59716-007-5 (lib. bdg.)—ISBN 1-59716-030-X (pbk.)
 1. Dust storms—Great Plains—Juvenile literature. 2. Droughts—Great Plains—Juvenile literature. 3. Dust storms—Great Plains—History—20th century—Juvenile literature. 4. Droughts—Great Plains—History—20th century—Juvenile literature. I. Title. II. Series.

 QC959.G73L49 2005
 363.34'929—dc22

                    2004020742

For more information, write to Bearport Publishing Company, Inc., 101 Fifth Avenue, Suite 6R, New York, New York 10003. Printed in the United States of America.

1 2 3 4 5 6 7 8 9 10

Table of Contents

Black Sunday

April 14, 1935, was a warm day in the **Great Plains** states. People were outside enjoying the sun and the bright sky. The day would have been perfect if the fields had not been so dry.

▼ This black blizzard hit Spearman, Texas, on April 14, 1935.

Suddenly, a huge black cloud covered the sun. It moved faster than a car racing down a street. The cloud roared across the fields. It swallowed up birds too slow to fly out of its way. The cloud was a storm filled with dirt. It was a deadly **black blizzard**. The day turned dark and cold. Black Sunday had begun.

On Black Sunday, the temperature fell 50 degrees in a few hours. The dust blocked the sun's heat and light.

Deadly Drifts

Melt White and his family were in their house. It was dark. Melt held his hand up to his face. He couldn't see it until his fingers touched his nose. The winds pounded the house. Dust flew in through cracks in the wall. Melt's father left footprints in the dust when he walked across the room.

◀ Garden City, Kansas, just before a dust storm hits in 1935

Outside, some people were trapped in their cars. The wind blew the dry soil off the ground. The soil piled up into large **drifts**. The dust was very fine. People would not be able to breathe if they fell into a drift.

▼ Garden City, Kansas, during a dust storm in 1935. This picture was taken 15 minutes after the photo on page 6 was shot.

The Dust Bowl

The next day, the land had been **reshaped** by the wind. A reporter thought the land looked like the Rose Bowl in California. He called it the **Dust Bowl**. The name stuck.

▲ The "red" states were the ones most often hit by the black blizzards.

There had been many black blizzards in the 1930s, but many believed Black Sunday was the worst. The storms could cover whole towns with dust clouds. People felt like they were drowning in dust. They tied wet handkerchiefs over their faces so they could breathe. The dust, however, still got into their mouths and noses. It hurt their eyes. Many got sick and others died.

◀ These women hold handkerchiefs over their faces during a dust storm in Missouri in 1935.

There were so many black blizzards between 1930 and 1939 that some people called that time "The Dirty 30s."

Dangerous Farming

What caused these **dust storms**? In the 1920s, many farmers had moved to the Great Plains. They pulled up the native grasses and cut down the trees to plant **crops**. The farmers didn't know that the grass roots were helping to hold the soil in place. They didn't understand how much the trees slowed the wind from racing over the flat ground.

Farmers also let their animals wander the land. They ate most of the plants. Soon the soil was loose. There was nothing to hold it down.

The Dust Bowl Years

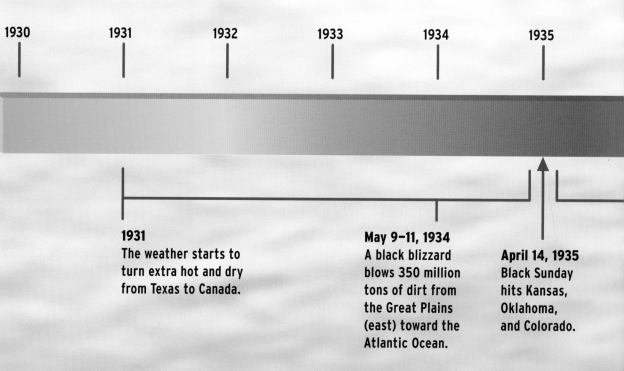

1930 1931 1932 1933 1934 1935

1931
The weather starts to turn extra hot and dry from Texas to Canada.

May 9–11, 1934
A black blizzard blows 350 million tons of dirt from the Great Plains (east) toward the Atlantic Ocean.

April 14, 1935
Black Sunday hits Kansas, Oklahoma, and Colorado.

In March 1935, 12 straight days of dust storms destroyed nearly half of the wheat crop in Kansas.

◀ The land in South Dakota was very dry in 1936.

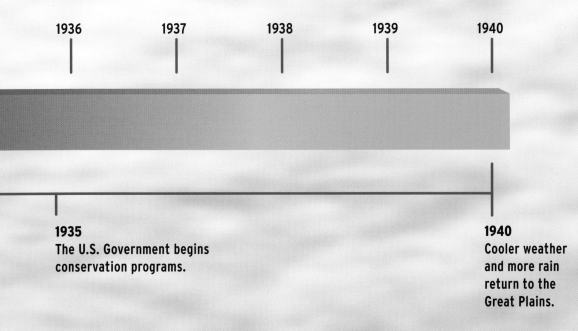

1936   1937   1938   1939   1940

1935
The U.S. Government begins conservation programs.

1940
Cooler weather and more rain return to the Great Plains.

Dry as Dust

In the 1930s, a long dry period called a **drought** began in the Great Plains. The land looked like a desert. The streams dried up and the rivers got smaller. Wells were empty or full of dirt. In Fort Smith, Arkansas, a reporter was told people couldn't drink the water because it was dirty. It was making them sick when they brushed their teeth with it.

▼ A farm in Texas after a black blizzard

The loose dirt became even drier and very light. When farmers **plowed** the dusty fields, the winds picked up the loose dirt and carried it away. This dirt helped start the black blizzards.

During the drought, dust storms destroyed most farms in a 400-mile-long, 300-mile-wide area.

13

It Was Hot!

The weather was also very hot during the mid-1930s. In many Dust Bowl states, daytime temperatures stayed above 100°F for a month at a time.

▲ In North Dakota, a family stuffed their windows with towels and clothing to keep out the dust.

The sun baked the people along with the land. There were no air conditioners back then. A few families had electricity to run fans. All the fans did, however, was stir the hot air. People couldn't even open their windows because the dust would blow inside. There also wasn't enough water for people to keep cool.

▲ In 1936, the earth in South Dakota was so dry that it cracked.

In Oklahoma City, Oklahoma, the average temperature in August is about 81°F. In 1936, it reached 113°F.

Not Just People

Animals **suffered**, too. The dust covered the cows' eyes. Their tears turned the dust to mud. When the mud dried, it sealed their eyes shut. Then they walked blindly into fences. They often died because they couldn't find any food or water.

Cows trying to get water from a watering hole that is almost dry in Oklahoma in 1936

Certain insects did fine in the hot dry weather. Billions of grasshoppers were hatched. They ate every blade of grass, including most of the wheat that farmers had planted. When they were finished, people had very little to eat. Now people feared they might die because they didn't have enough food.

During the Dust Bowl, many of the animals that would have eaten the grasshoppers died. They didn't have enough water or food.

The Dust Bowl Sweeps a Nation

The number of black blizzards grew each year in the mid-1930s. Outside the Dust Bowl, however, nobody seemed to notice. The U.S. was in the **Great Depression**. Millions of people were out of work. Government leaders had lots to worry about. Besides, black blizzards happened far from the nation's **capital**.

Then, from May 9–11, 1934, wild winds blew dirt from the Great Plains all the way to Washington, D.C. A newspaper reported that one cloud of dust was 1,500 miles long, 900 miles across, and 2 miles high. The cloud covered a large part of the nation. Now, leaders paid attention.

▼ Washington, D.C. before the dust storm hit

In May 1934, even ships 300 miles out in the Atlantic Ocean were covered in dirt.

A Better Way

A government **official** named Hugh Hammond Bennett knew that the dust storms were the result of bad farming practices. Bennett had been born in North Carolina. His father was a cotton planter. He understood farms and how to care for the soil.

◄ Hugh Hammond Bennett taught farm families better ways to take care of the land.

Bennett sent workers to the Dust Bowl to teach the farmers better ways of plowing and planting. They told the farmers to plant trees to slow the wind. The workers gave the farmers seeds for special kinds of grass that didn't need much water. They also taught them how to save water.

▲ Hugh Hammond Bennett (right) discussing farming practices

The government paid farmers NOT to grow certain crops. They told farmers to grow grass until the dust problem was under control.

Heading West

Some farmers stayed and changed to the new ways. They were proud people who hadn't meant to cause the dust problem. Melt White's family stayed and did well.

Other people could not stay. They had no money. There was nothing to eat and no way for anyone to make a living. Between 1931 and 1939, more than two and a half million farmers and their families packed up and left the Great Plains. They sold everything they owned. Many went to California where crops were still growing. They might still get farm work there.

Many of the people who left the Dust Bowl were from Oklahoma. They became known as "Okies."

Keep Out!

Families piled into old cars or trucks and drove through the blazing heat. They camped by the road at night. When they reached California, the lucky ones got jobs on farms or in factories. The pay was low. They had to live without running water or electricity. They had to move around to find work. Few kids went to school.

▼ Eighty Dust Bowl families lived in this auto camp in California.

Soon, California said it was running out of room. In 1936, the Los Angeles chief of police sent officers to **patrol** California's borders with Arizona and Oregon. The unlucky families were turned away.

◀ A Dust Bowl family

Newspapers called the policemen who were turning people away at the borders "The Bum Brigade."

An End and a Beginning

By 1939, the drought was over. Rain fell in the Dust Bowl. The country began to **recover** from the Great Depression. President Franklin D. Roosevelt started programs to help people. Now there were ways to earn money and get food and clothes.

▼ President Franklin D. Roosevelt

In the Dust Bowl, trees and grass grew again. The soil stayed put. The wind slowed down. Farmers planted their crops using water-saving plans.

There hasn't been a black blizzard since the 1930s. Today the Great Plains states supply most of the wheat and corn used in the United States. It's once again the nation's **breadbasket**.

▼ Healthy crops grow where there was once dust.

The United States produced about 11.6 billion bushels of corn in 2004. Corn can be used to make fuel, clothing, and plastics.

Just the Facts

Black Sunday

- Before the cloud appeared, thousands of birds flew into people's yards. They were flapping their wings in fear.
- The black cloud was full of electricity. The electricity caused cars to stop working. Many got stuck in the middle of the road.
- During the storm, ten people were trapped in a small hut. It was so dark they couldn't see each other.

Black Blizzards

- In March 1935, a dust storm in Colorado left so much dirt on the railroad tracks that a train jumped off the track.
- One black blizzard in May 1934 carried 350 tons of dirt. Around 12 million tons fell over the city of Chicago.
- Sometimes snow mixed with the dust during the winter. People called that kind of storm a "snuster."

Changes in America caused by the Dust Bowl

- President Roosevelt signed a law that said state groups had to look after natural resources.
- Farmers learned to stop cattle and sheep from eating all the grasses that hold the soil in place.
- Scientists now make mini dust storms in labs to study their effect on the land.

◄ A dust storm hits Amarillo, Texas in 1936.

Glossary

black blizzard (BLAK BLIZ-urd)   a windstorm in which tons of loose dirt, dust, and soil are blown around in a thick cloud

breadbasket (BRED-*bass*-kit)   the place that supplies most of the grain (corn and wheat) for an area

capital (kap-UH-tuhl)   the city in a state or country where the government is located

crops (KROPS)   plants grown and gathered, often for food

drifts (DRIFTS)   piles created by the wind

drought (drout)   a long period of dry weather

Dust Bowl (DUST *bohl*)   a very dry area that stretched through the central United States in the 1930s

dust storms (DUST *stormz*)   huge windstorms that blow dust and dirt across many miles

Great Depression (GRAYT di-PRESH-uhn)   the period from 1929 through the 1930's when many people in the U.S. lost their money, jobs, businesses, and farms

Great Plains (GRAYT PLAYNZ)   a large, grassland region of central North America

official (uh-FISH-uhl)   a person who holds an office or important position

patrol (puh-TROHL)   to travel around an area to guard it and keep watch on people

plowed (PLOUD)   soil that has been turned over using a piece of farm equipment called a plow

recover (ri-KUHV-ur)   to get better after a difficult period

reshaped (ree-SHAYPD)   molded into a new shape

suffered (SUHF-urd)   felt pain

Bibliography

Stallings, Frank L. *Black Sunday: The Great Dust Storm of April 14, 1935.* Austin, TX: Eakin Press (2001).

Svobida, Lawrence. *Farming the Dust Bowl: A First-Hand Account from Kansas.* Lawrence, KS: University Press of Kansas (1986).

Worster, Donald. *Dust Bowl: The Southern Plains in the 1930s.* New York, NY: Oxford University Press (1979).

Read More

Booth, Michael, and Karen Reczuch. *The Dust Bowl.* Toronto, Canada: Kids Can Press (1997).

Connell, Kate. *Hoping for Rain: The Dust Bowl Adventures of Patty and Earl Buckler.* Washington, D.C.: National Geographic (2004).

Isaacs, Sally Senzell. *Life in the Dust Bowl (Picture the Past).* Chicago, IL: Heinemann Library (2001).

Learn More Online

Visit these Web sites to learn more about the Dust Bowl and farming:

- www.livinghistoryfarm.org
- www.pbs.org/wgbh/amex/dustbowl/peopleevents/pandeAMEX07.html
- www.planetbookclub.com/teachers/dust.html
- www.ptsi.net/user/museum/dustbowl.html

Index

About the Author

Richard H. Levey is a senior writer for *Direct*, a New York-based marketing magazine. Even though he makes his home in New York, he lives in fear of black blizzards.